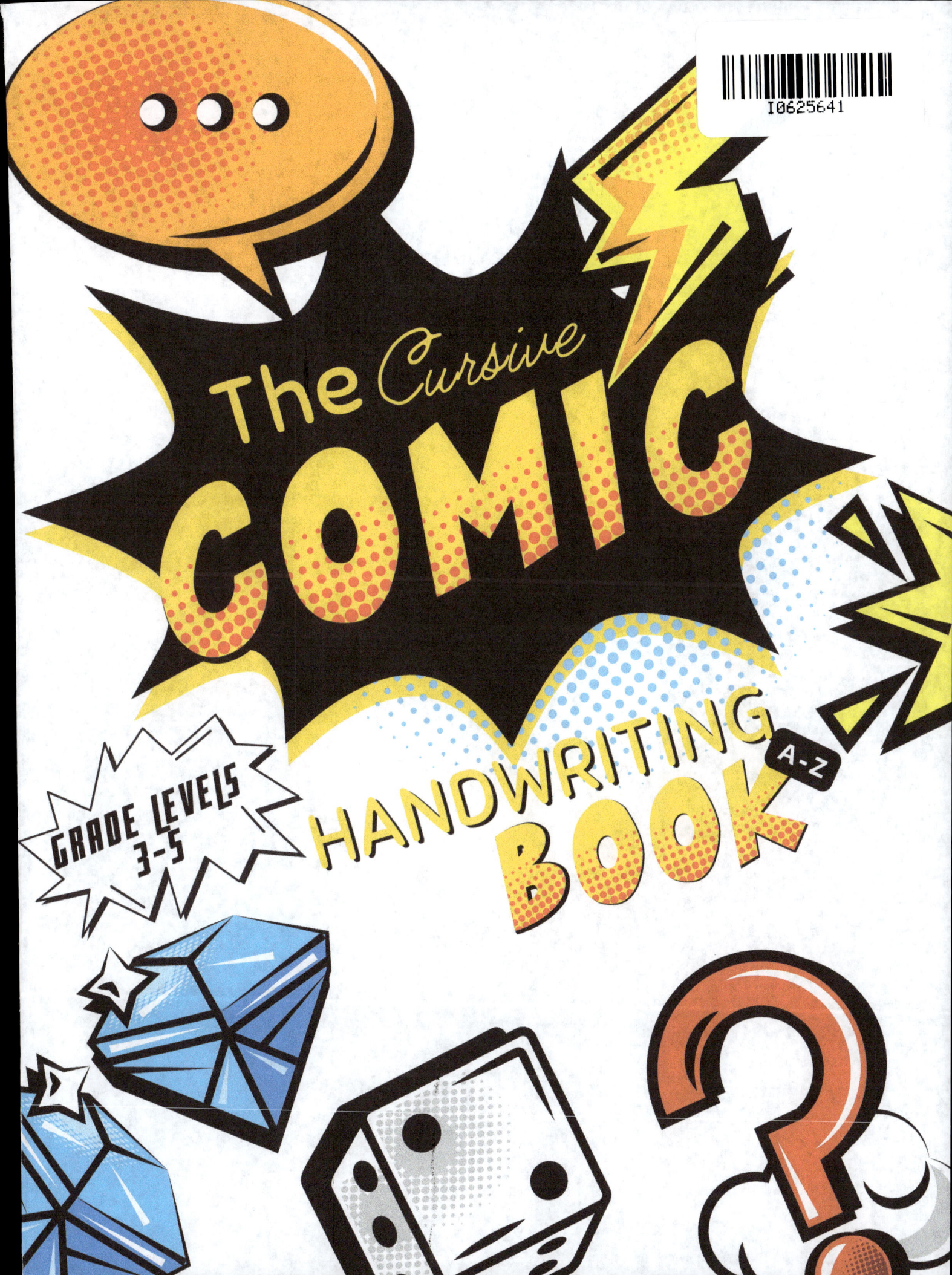

PUBLISHING

"If better is possible, good is not enough."
— Benjamin Franklin

Published by: EarKanDee LLC
For more information: earkandee.educate@gmail.com
ISBN: 979-8-9989132-2-8
www.earkandeeonline.com

*To my husband,*
*Your hard work, perseverance, and dedication is heroic.*

# TABLE OF CONTENTS

| MONDAY | TUESDAY | WEDNESDAY | THURSDAY | FRIDAY |
|--------|---------|-----------|----------|--------|
|        |         |           |          |        |
|        |         |           |          |        |
|        |         |           |          |        |
|        |         |           |          |        |

## UPPERCASE

A B C D E
F G H I J
K L M
N O P
Q R S
T U V W
X Y Z

LET'S SEE IF THEY CAN COMPLETE THE MISSION SUCCESSFULLY.

I CREATED QUITE THE CHALLENGE.

**VS**

a b c d e
f g h i j
k l m
n o p
q r s
t u v w
x y z

THEY WILL NOT GIVE UP!

WE WILL COMPLETE THE MISSION TOGETHER!

## LOWERCASE

PRACTICE WRITING THE UPPER AND LOWERCASE LETTERS IN CURSIVE.

*Aa*

*Aa*

*Aa*

PRACTICE WRITING THE WORD IN CURSIVE.

*amazing*

YOU CAN DO IT!

YEAH!

PRACTICE WRITING THE SENTENCE IN CURSIVE.

*You are amazing!*

3

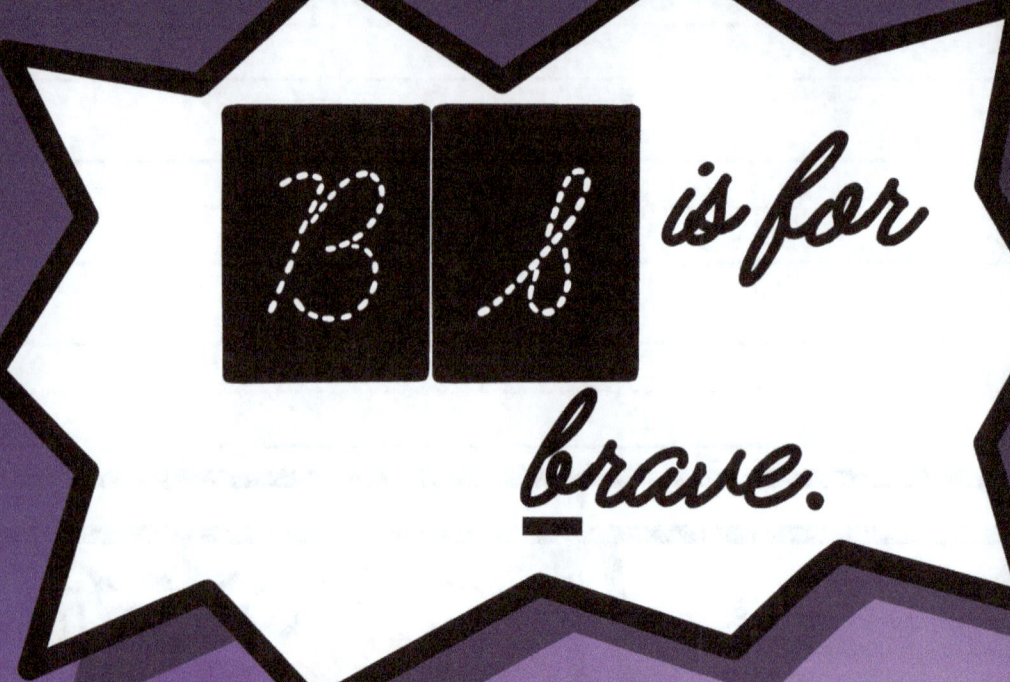

NEVER FEAR!
THE HEROS OF
HANDWRITING
ARE HERE!

HELP!

HELP!

HELP!

4

PRACTICE WRITING THE UPPER AND LOWERCASE LETTERS IN CURSIVE.

*Bb*

*Bb*

*Bb*

PRACTICE WRITING THE WORD IN CURSIVE.

*brave*

I BELIEVE IN YOU!

COOL!

PRACTICE WRITING THE SENTENCE IN CURSIVE.

*Brave people are cool!*

5

PRACTICE WRITING THE UPPER AND LOWERCASE LETTERS IN CURSIVE.

*Cc*

*Cc*

*Cc*

PRACTICE WRITING THE WORD IN CURSIVE.

*courageous*

NEVER GIVE UP!

WOW!

PRACTICE WRITING THE SENTENCE IN CURSIVE.

*I am courageous!*

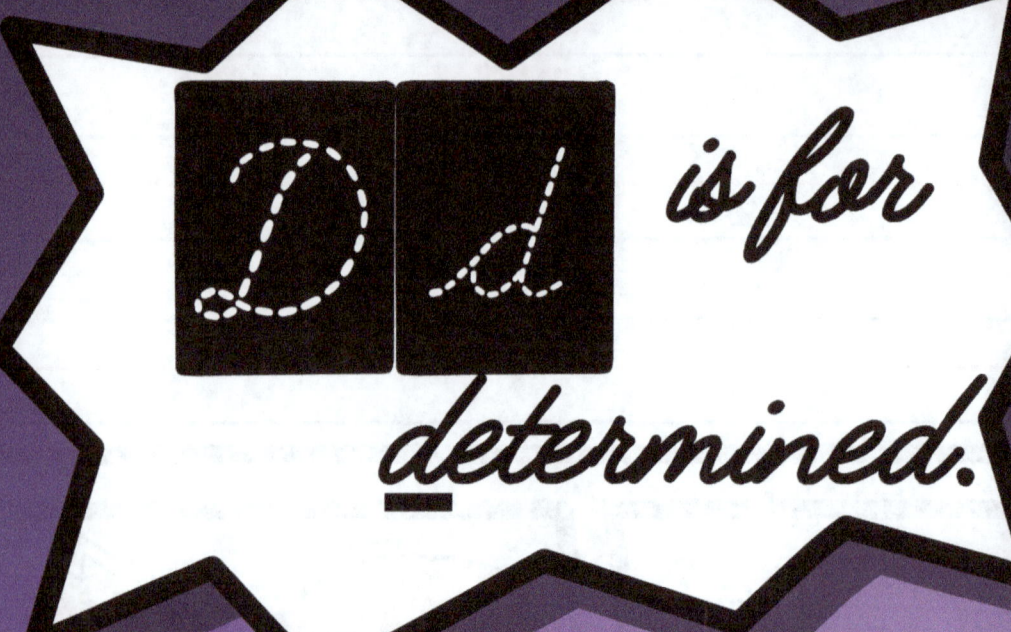

**Dd** is for <u>determined</u>.

NEVER FEAR! THE HEROS OF HANDWRITING ARE HERE!

HELP!

HELP!

HELP!

PRACTICE WRITING THE UPPER AND LOWERCASE LETTERS IN CURSIVE.

*Dd*

*Dd*

*Dd*

PRACTICE WRITING THE WORD IN CURSIVE.

*determined*

YOU CAN DO IT!

YEAH!

PRACTICE WRITING THE SENTENCE IN CURSIVE.

*We are determined!*

PRACTICE WRITING THE UPPER AND LOWERCASE LETTERS IN CURSIVE.

*Ee*

*Ee*

*Ee*

PRACTICE WRITING THE WORD IN CURSIVE.

*exceptional*

I BELIEVE IN YOU!

COOL!

PRACTICE WRITING THE SENTENCE IN CURSIVE.

*You are exceptional!*

11

**Ff** is for *fearless.*

NEVER FEAR! THE HEROS OF HANDWRITING ARE HERE!

HELP!

HELP!

HELP!

12

# PRACTICE WRITING THE UPPER AND LOWERCASE LETTERS IN CURSIVE.

*Ff*

*Ff*

*Ff*

## PRACTICE WRITING THE WORD IN CURSIVE.

*fearless*

NEVER GIVE UP!

WOW!

## PRACTICE WRITING THE SENTENCE IN CURSIVE.

*I am fearless!*

13

14

PRACTICE WRITING THE UPPER AND LOWERCASE LETTERS IN CURSIVE.

*Gg*

*Gg*

*Gg*

PRACTICE WRITING THE WORD IN CURSIVE.

*gracious*

YOU CAN DO IT!

YEAH!

PRACTICE WRITING THE SENTENCE IN CURSIVE.

*We are gracious.*

15

**Hh** is for <u>h</u>eroic.

NEVER FEAR! THE HEROS OF HANDWRITING ARE HERE!

HELP!

HELP!

HELP!

16

PRACTICE WRITING THE UPPER AND LOWERCASE LETTERS IN CURSIVE.

*Hh*

*Hh*

*Hh*

PRACTICE WRITING THE WORD IN CURSIVE.

*heroic*

I BELIEVE IN YOU!

COOL!

PRACTICE WRITING THE SENTENCE IN CURSIVE.

*You are heroic!*

*I i* is for invincible.

NEVER FEAR! WE ARE HERE TO LEAD THE WAY!

HELP!

HELP!

HELP!

PRACTICE WRITING THE UPPER AND LOWERCASE LETTERS IN CURSIVE.

*Ii*

*Ii*

*Ii*

PRACTICE WRITING THE WORD IN CURSIVE.

*invincible*

NEVER GIVE UP!

WOW!

PRACTICE WRITING THE SENTENCE IN CURSIVE.

*I am invincible!*

PRACTICE WRITING THE UPPER AND LOWERCASE LETTERS IN CURSIVE.

*J j*

*J j*

*J j*

PRACTICE WRITING THE WORD IN CURSIVE.

*jubilant*

YOU CAN DO IT!

YEAH!

PRACTICE WRITING THE SENTENCE IN CURSIVE.

*We are jubilant.*

**K k** is for **kind.**

PRACTICE WRITING THE UPPER AND LOWERCASE LETTERS IN CURSIVE.

*Kk*

*Kk*

*Kk*

PRACTICE WRITING THE WORD IN CURSIVE.

*kind*

I BELIEVE IN YOU!

COOL!

PRACTICE WRITING THE SENTENCE IN CURSIVE.

*You are kind.*

*Ll* is for **legendary**

NEVER FEAR!
THE HEROS OF
HANDWRITING
ARE HERE!

HELP!

HELP!

HELP!

PRACTICE WRITING THE UPPER AND LOWERCASE LETTERS IN CURSIVE.

*Ll*

*Ll*

*Ll*

PRACTICE WRITING THE WORD IN CURSIVE.

*legendary*

NEVER GIVE UP!

WOW!

PRACTICE WRITING THE SENTENCE IN CURSIVE.

*I am legendary!*

25

**Nn** is for **<u>m</u>ighty.**

PRACTICE WRITING THE UPPER AND LOWERCASE LETTERS IN CURSIVE.

*Mm*

*Mm*

*Mm*

PRACTICE WRITING THE WORD IN CURSIVE.

*mighty*

YOU CAN DO IT!

YEAH!

PRACTICE WRITING THE SENTENCE IN CURSIVE.

*We are mighty!*

Nn is for noble.
NEVER FEAR! THE HEROS OF HANDWRITING ARE HERE!
HELP!
HELP!
HELP!

PRACTICE WRITING THE UPPER AND LOWERCASE LETTERS IN CURSIVE.

*Nn*

*Nn*

*Nn*

PRACTICE WRITING THE WORD IN CURSIVE.

*noble*

I BELIEVE IN YOU!

COOL!

PRACTICE WRITING THE SENTENCE IN CURSIVE.

*You are noble!*

O o is for optimistic
NEVER FEAR! WE ARE HERE TO LEAD THE WAY!
HELP!
HELP!
HELP!

PRACTICE WRITING THE UPPER AND LOWERCASE LETTERS IN CURSIVE.

*Oo*

*Oo*

*Oo*

PRACTICE WRITING THE WORD IN CURSIVE.

*optimistic*

NEVER GIVE UP!

WOW!

PRACTICE WRITING THE SENTENCE IN CURSIVE.

*I am optimistic!*

32

PRACTICE WRITING THE UPPER AND LOWERCASE LETTERS IN CURSIVE.

*Pp*

*Pp*

*Pp*

PRACTICE WRITING THE WORD IN CURSIVE.

*powerful*

YOU CAN DO IT!

YEAH!

PRACTICE WRITING THE SENTENCE IN CURSIVE.

*We are powerful!*

Qq is for quick.

NEVER FEAR! WE ARE HERE TO LEAD THE WAY!

HELP!

HELP!

HELP!

34

PRACTICE WRITING THE UPPER AND LOWERCASE LETTERS IN CURSIVE.

*Qg*

*Qg*

*Qg*

PRACTICE WRITING THE WORD IN CURSIVE.

*quick*

I BELIEVE IN YOU!

COOL!

PRACTICE WRITING THE SENTENCE IN CURSIVE.

*You are quick!*

**Rr** is for _resilient.

NEVER FEAR!
THE HEROS OF
HANDWRITING
ARE HERE!

HELP!

HELP!

HELP!

PRACTICE WRITING THE UPPER AND LOWERCASE LETTERS IN CURSIVE.

*Rr*

*Rr*

*Rr*

PRACTICE WRITING THE WORD IN CURSIVE.

*resilient*

NEVER GIVE UP!

WOW!

PRACTICE WRITING THE SENTENCE IN CURSIVE.

*I am resilient!*

Ss is for super.

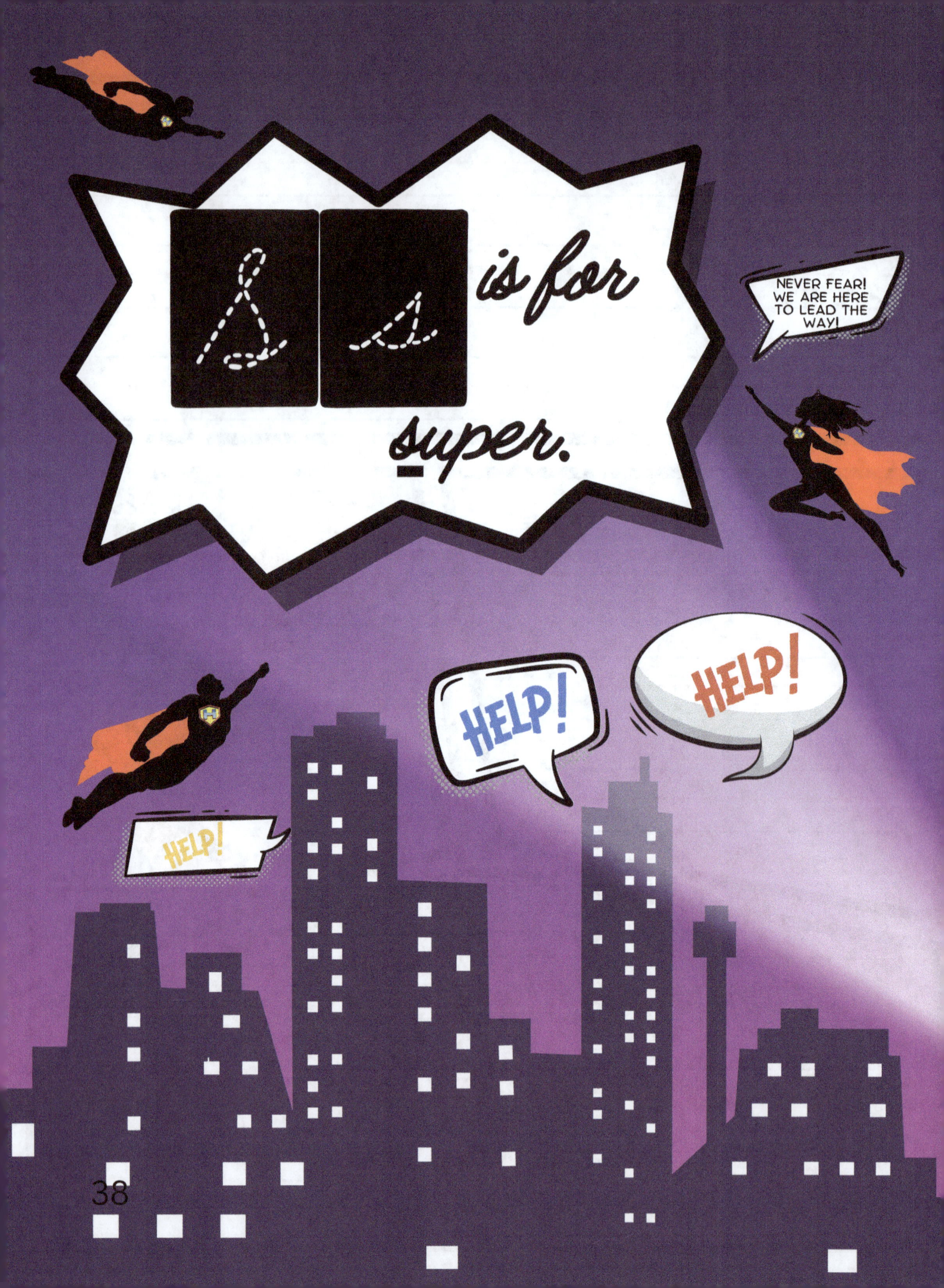

PRACTICE WRITING THE UPPER AND LOWERCASE LETTERS IN CURSIVE.

*Ss*

*Ss*

*Ss*

PRACTICE WRITING THE WORD IN CURSIVE.

*super*

YOU CAN DO IT!

YEAH!

PRACTICE WRITING THE SENTENCE IN CURSIVE.

*We are super!*

Tt is for tenacious.
NEVER FEAR! THE HEROS OF HANDWRITING ARE HERE!
HELP!
HELP!
HELP!

PRACTICE WRITING THE UPPER AND LOWERCASE LETTERS IN CURSIVE.

*T*

*T*

*T*

PRACTICE WRITING THE WORD IN CURSIVE.

*tenacious*

I BELIEVE IN YOU!

COOL!

PRACTICE WRITING THE SENTENCE IN CURSIVE.

*You are tenacious!*

41

*U u* is for <u>u</u>nstoppable.

PRACTICE WRITING THE UPPER AND LOWERCASE LETTERS IN CURSIVE.

*Uu*

*Uu*

*Uu*

PRACTICE WRITING THE WORD IN CURSIVE.

*unstoppable*

NEVER GIVE UP!

WOW!

PRACTICE WRITING THE SENTENCE IN CURSIVE.

*I am unstoppable!*

V v is for valiant.
NEVER FEAR! THE HEROS OF HANDWRITING ARE HERE!
HELP!
HELP!
HELP!

PRACTICE WRITING THE UPPER AND LOWERCASE LETTERS IN CURSIVE.

*Vv*

*Vv*

*Vv*

PRACTICE WRITING THE WORD IN CURSIVE.

*valiant*

YOU CAN DO IT!

YEAH!

PRACTICE WRITING THE SENTENCE IN CURSIVE.

*We are valiant.*

W w is for

wise.

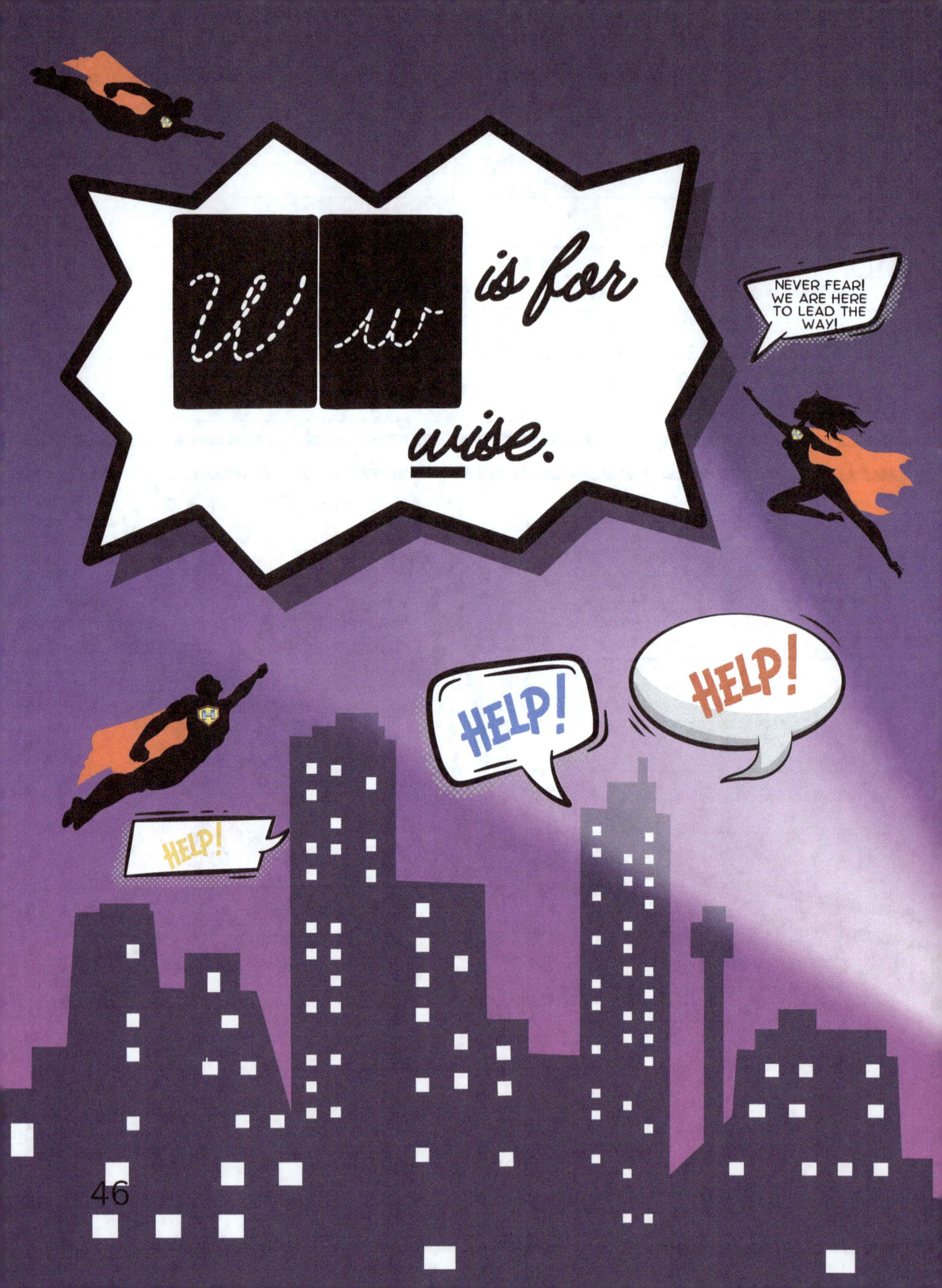

PRACTICE WRITING THE UPPER AND LOWERCASE LETTERS IN CURSIVE.

*Ww*

*Ww*

*Ww*

PRACTICE WRITING THE WORD IN CURSIVE.

*wise*

I BELIEVE IN YOU!

COOL!

PRACTICE WRITING THE SENTENCE IN CURSIVE.

*You are wise!*

# Xx is for xenial.

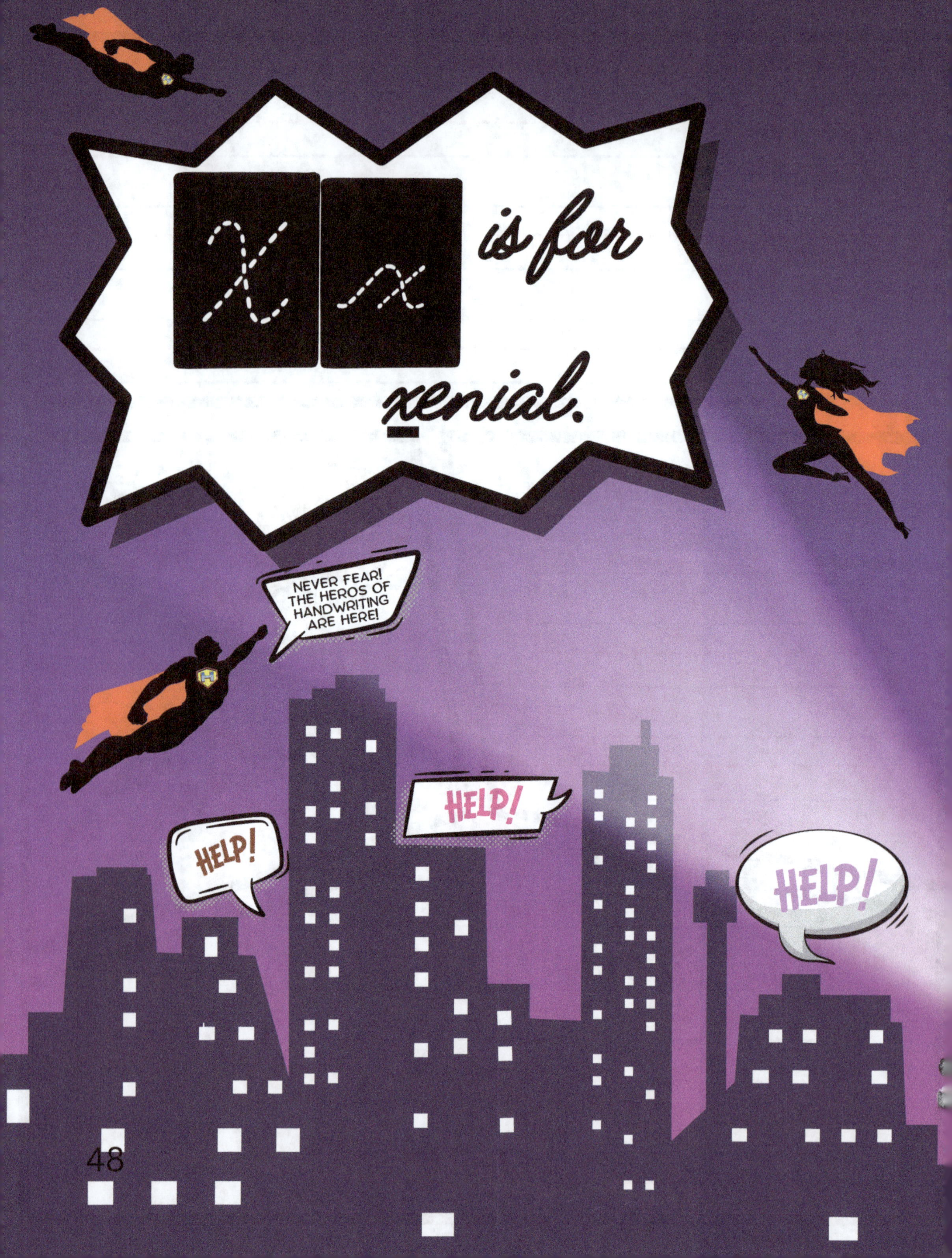

PRACTICE WRITING THE UPPER AND LOWERCASE LETTERS IN CURSIVE.

*Xx*

*Xx*

*Xx*

PRACTICE WRITING THE WORD IN CURSIVE.

*xenial*

NEVER GIVE UP!

WOW!

PRACTICE WRITING THE SENTENCE IN CURSIVE.

*I am xenial.*

Y y is for youthful.
NEVER FEAR! WE ARE HERE TO LEAD THE WAY!
HELP!
HELP!
HELP!

PRACTICE WRITING THE UPPER AND LOWERCASE LETTERS IN CURSIVE.

*Yy*

*Yy*

*Yy*

PRACTICE WRITING THE WORD IN CURSIVE.

*youthful*

YOU CAN DO IT!

YEAH!

PRACTICE WRITING THE SENTENCE IN CURSIVE.

*We are youthful.*

PRACTICE WRITING THE UPPER AND LOWERCASE LETTERS IN CURSIVE.

*Zz*

*Zz*

*Zz*

PRACTICE WRITING THE WORD IN CURSIVE.

*zealous*

I BELIEVE IN YOU!

COOL!

PRACTICE WRITING THE SENTENCE IN CURSIVE.

*You are zealous!*

# EARKANDEE
# LLC

## LISTEN | DESIGN | DISCOVER

## PUBLISHING "EFFECTIVE"
## EDUCATIONAL RESOURCES GLOBALLY

# NOW ON AMAZON

| | | | |
|---|---|---|---|
| **"MUST LEARN SIGHTWORDS" THROUGH READING, WRITING, AND MATH WORKBOOK (KINDERGARTEN)** *AVAILABLE NOW* | **"MUST LEARN SIGHTWORDS" THROUGH READING, WRITING, AND MATH WORKBOOK (FIRST GRADE)** *AVAILABLE NOW* | **"MUST LEARN SIGHTWORDS" THROUGH READING, WRITING, AND MATH WORKBOOK (SECOND GRADE)** *AVAILABLE NOW* | **MY FIRST COUNTING IN SPACE BOOK** *AVAILABLE NOW* |
| **MATH "GROWTH" JOURNAL GRADE LEVELS K-5** *AVAILABLE NOW* | **MATH "GROWTH" JOURNAL GRADE LEVELS 6-8** *AVAILABLE NOW* | **MATH "GROWTH" JOURNAL GRADE LEVELS 9-12** *AVAILABLE NOW* | **MY FIRST COUNTING IN SPORTS BOOK** *AVAILABLE NOW* |
| **WRITING ON THE ROADS OF THE USA "STATES": K-2 HANDWRITING WORKBOOK** *AVAILABLE NOW* | **G.R.E.A.T. IS FOR A DAY WITH MY GRANDPARENTS! CHILDREN'S BOOK** *AVAILABLE NOW* | **THE MIGHTY MOVE UPSTAIRS CHILDREN'S BOOK** *AVAILABLE NOW* | **MY FIRST COUNTING WITH MERMAIDS BOOK** *AVAILABLE NOW* |
| **MY FIRST COUNTING WITH JUNGLE ANIMALS BOOK** *AVAILABLE NOW* | **THE PRINCESS PALETTE COLORING BOOK** *AVAILABLE NOW* | **THE COUNTING MERMAIDS CHILDREN'S BOOK** *AVAILABLE NOW* | **MY FIRST COUNTING IN THE SNOW BOOK** *AVAILABLE NOW* |
| **THE MERMAID PALETTE COLORING BOOK** *AVAILABLE NOW* | **MY FIRST COUNTING IN CAREERS BOOK** *AVAILABLE NOW* | **MY FIRST COUNTING WITH MONEY BOOK** *AVAILABLE NOW* | **THE COLOR COLLAGE COLORING BOOK A-Z** *AVAILABLE NOW* |

*Stay Tuned For More....*

**DON'T FORGET TO**
WRITE A REVIEW
ON AMAZON

Find us at:

**www.earkandeeonline.com**

Contact us:

**earkandee.educate@gmail.com**